ROSEN *Verified*

NATURAL DISASTERS

TSUNAMIS

Jennifer Lombardo

ROSEN PUBLISHING

Published in 2023 by The Rosen Publishing Group, Inc.
2544 Clinton Street, Buffalo, NY 14224

First Edition

Editor: Greg Roza
Book Design: Michael Flynn

Photo Credits: Cover Erlantz P.R/Shutterstock.com; (series background) PinkPueblo/Shutterstock.com; p. 5 Volina/Shutterstock.com; p. 7 Michael Vi/Shutterstock.com; p. 8 (wave artwork) Arif_S/Shutterstock.com; p. 9 (ocean) Oskari Porkka/Shutterstock.com; p. 11 Elenarts/Shutterstock.com; p. 12 Kolonko/Shutterstock.com; pp. 13, 15 VectorMine/Shutterstock.com; p. 14 vchal/Shutterstock.com; p. 16 zizou7/Shutterstock.com; p. 17 J.A. Dunbar/Shutterstock.com; p. 19 Knoph Photography/Shutterstock.com; p. 21 T.P. Walker/NOAA; p. 22 Evgeniia Engkilterra/Shutterstock.com; p. 23 ultrapok/Shutterstock.com; p. 25 mTaira/Shutterstock.com; p. 26 speedshutter Photography/Shutterstock.com; p. 27 1000 Words.Shutterstock.com; p. 29 https://commons.wikimedia.org/wiki/File:Distant_view_of_Rikuzentakata.jpg; p. 30 tunasalmon/Shutterstock.com; p. 31LukaKikina/Shutterstock.com; p. 33 Sadatsugu Tomizawa/JPL NASA; p. 34 Sabina Zak/Shutterstock; p. 35 https://commons.wikimedia.org/wiki/File:US_Navy_050102-N-9593M-040_A_village_near_the_coast_of_Sumatra_lays_in_ruin_after_the_Tsunami_that_struck_South_East_Asia.jpg; p. 37 La Bella Studio/Shutterstock.com; p. 39 Youkonton/Shutterstock.com; p. 41 Frans Delian/Shutterstock.com; p. 42 https://commons.wikimedia.org/wiki/File:Fuel_Assembly_Removal_Process_(02813602).jpg; p. 43 Falcon video/Shutterstock.com; p. 45 Marijs/Shutterstock.com.

Cataloging-in-Publication Data

Names: Lombardo, Jennifer
Title: Tsunamis, Jennifer Lombardo
Description: New York: Rosen Publishing, [2023] | Series: Rosen Verified : Natural Disasters | Includes index.
Identifiers: LCCN | ISBN: 9781499473575 (library binding) | 9781499473568 (paperback) | 9781499473582 (ebook)
Subjects: LCSH: Tsunamis - Juvenile literature
Classifications: LCC: GC221.5 | DDC 551.46

Manufactured in the United States of America

Some of the images in this book illustrate individuals who are models. The depictions do not imply actual situations or events.

CPSIA Compliance Information: Batch #CWRYA23. For further information contact Rosen Publishing at 1-800-237-9932.

CONTENTS

KNOWLEDGE IS POWER

It's normal to see waves in the ocean. However, some waves are more dangerous, or unsafe, than others. A tsunami is a series of huge ocean waves. Each wave can be up to 100 feet (30.5 m) tall.

Tsunamis don't happen very often. In the Pacific **Basin**, there are one or two every year. Tsunamis that affect the entire Pacific Basin happen once every 10 to 12 years. Some natural disasters happen more often at certain times of the year. For example, the Atlantic Basin has hurricane season every year between June and November. However, there is no tsunami season. This means people who live in places where a tsunami is likely to hit always need to be prepared.

The Pacific Basin includes all the countries around the edge of the Pacific Ocean as well as the islands in the ocean.

Tsunamis cause a lot of **damage** and death. Learning about them is the best way to stay safe. This is true for people who live in tsunami zones as well as those who just want to visit. Understanding how tsunamis are formed, the warning signs when one is about to hit, and what to do when it happens are all important things to learn and remember.

SPEEDING TSUNAMIS

Tsunami waves can travel thousands of miles very quickly. In the open ocean, with nothing in their way, they can reach speeds of 500 miles (804 km) per hour. When a fast-moving tsunami hits the shore, not much can stand in its way.

Regular waves are mostly caused by wind over the ocean. Their top speed is 56 miles (90 km) per hour. These waves don't damage much more than the sandcastles people build on the beach.

THAT'S FAST!

PERSON / ANIMAL / OBJECT	TOP SPEED
Usain Bolt	27.4 mph (44 kph)
cheetah	59 mph (95 kph)
hummingbird	61 mph (98 kph)
Hennessey Venom GT sports car	270 mph (435 kph)
tsunami wave	500 mph (804 kph)
Boeing 747-400 airplane	656 mph (1,056 kph)

The word "tsunami" means "great harbor wave" in Japanese.

DIFFERENT KINDS OF WAVES

The waves we would call "normal" are called wind waves by scientists. Strong winds that blow for a long time over a long distance form a kind of wave called a swell.

One kind of dangerous wave is called a **rogue** wave. It forms when swelling waves join together. Rogue waves seem to come out of nowhere. They're more than twice the size of the waves around them. People who see rogue waves are usually on ships far out in the ocean.

This painting, titled "The Great Wave off Kanagawa," was created around 1830 by artist Katsushika Hokusai. People who study art say this famous picture shows a rogue wave.

BEACHED BY A ROGUE WAVE

The Riverdance cargo ferry was hit by a rogue wave in 2008 and the ship was pushed onto the shore of Blackpool, England. Everyone who had been onboard was safely rescued.

WHY DO TSUNAMIS HAPPEN?

Tsunamis happen when a **disturbance** makes the ocean floor move suddenly. This movement causes water to be quickly displaced, or moved out of the way. Underwater earthquakes are the most common disturbance. Volcanoes and landslides can also cause tsunamis.

Millions of years ago, the **asteroid** that likely killed the dinosaurs also caused a tsunami. Scientists say it could have been as much as 1 mile (1.6 km) high. It would have covered everything but the tops of mountains for thousands of miles.

FAST FACT

Tsunamis used to be called "tidal waves." Today, we know they don't have anything to do with Earth's tides.

VERIFIED
Read more about the tsunami that was caused by the dinosaur-killing asteroid at **www.livescience.com/64426-dinosaur-killing-asteroid-caused-giant-tsunami.html.**

A massive asteroid landed near the Yucatan peninsula 65.5 million years ago. It created the Chicxulub Crater on Mexico's Gulf Coast. This astetroid strike is the most likely theory explaining how the dinosaurs were killed off.

CAUSE AND EFFECT

Earthquakes happen very often. They can happen on land or underwater. We don't feel most of them, but some of them cause a lot of damage. Earthquakes happen because the **lithosphere** is split into pieces called tectonic plates. The plates float on a layer of soft, liquid rock called magma.

EARTH'S TECTONIC PLATES

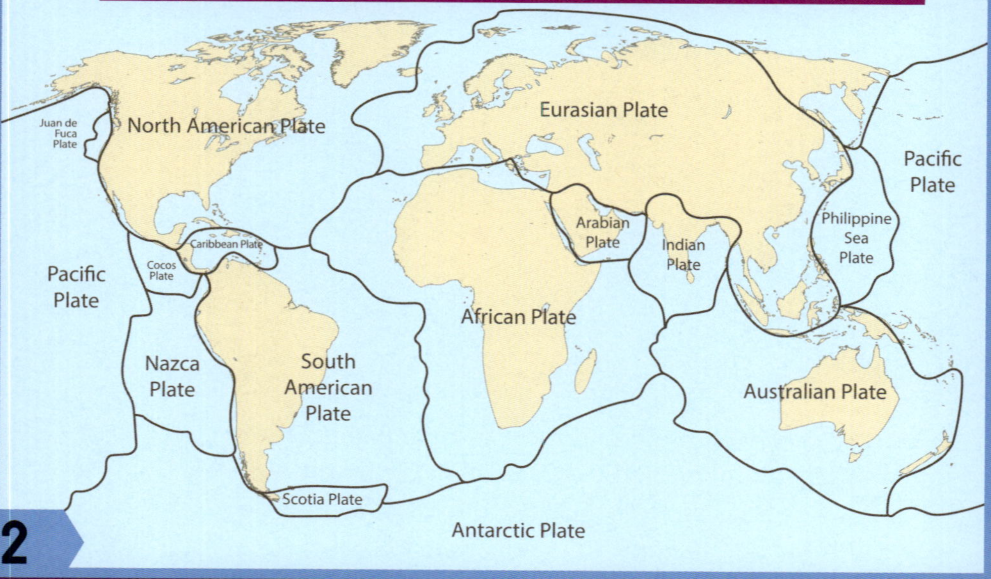

Tectonic plates are always moving. Sometimes they slide apart or move together. Other times, they slip past each other, grinding their way into a new position.

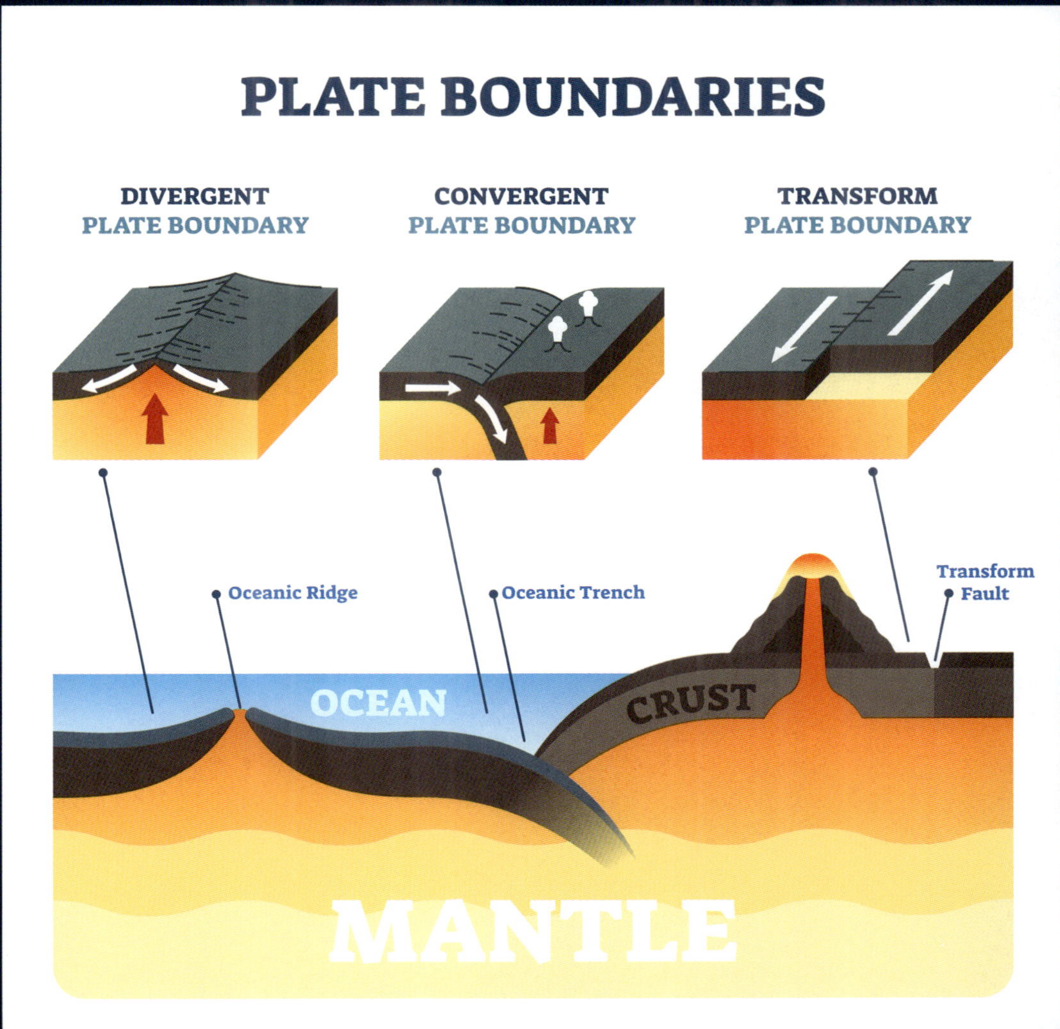

This picture shows the different ways plates move.

All of the movement of tectonic plates causes **pressure** to build up. When the pressure is released suddenly, an earthquake happens. When a big earthquake happens underwater, plates may move over or under each other. This sudden movement can displace a lot of water and cause a tsunami.

An earthquake in the middle of the ocean may drop or lift the ocean floor. This movement makes the water rise and form a wave. As the wave travels toward the shore, it picks up speed.

Seismologists have special equipment to record earthquakes.

VERIFIED

Scientists at the National Oceanic and Atmospheric Administration (NOAA) study and explain how tsunamis form. Learn more at **https://www.noaa.gov/education/resource-collections/ocean-coasts/tsunamis**.

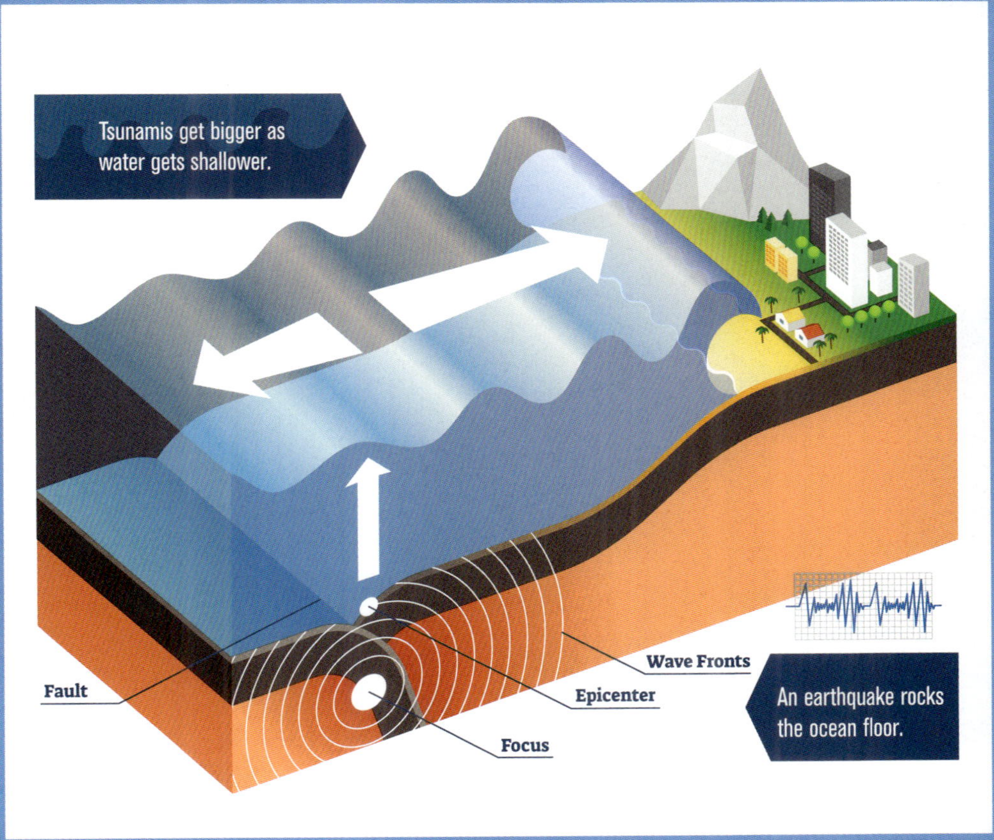

FAST FACT

The deeper the water is where the earthquake happens, the faster a tsunami travels. This is because the waves are formed by gravity rather than wind.

JUST THE BEGINNING

In the open ocean, a tsunami looks like regular waves. The water rises only about 3 feet (0.9 m) higher than usual. A tsunami can travel for thousands of miles this way.

As the waves move into **shallower** water, they start to slow down and build to greater heights. The top, or crest, of each wave moves faster than the bottom, or trough. This makes them grow taller very quickly. However, even small tsunamis can do a lot of damage.

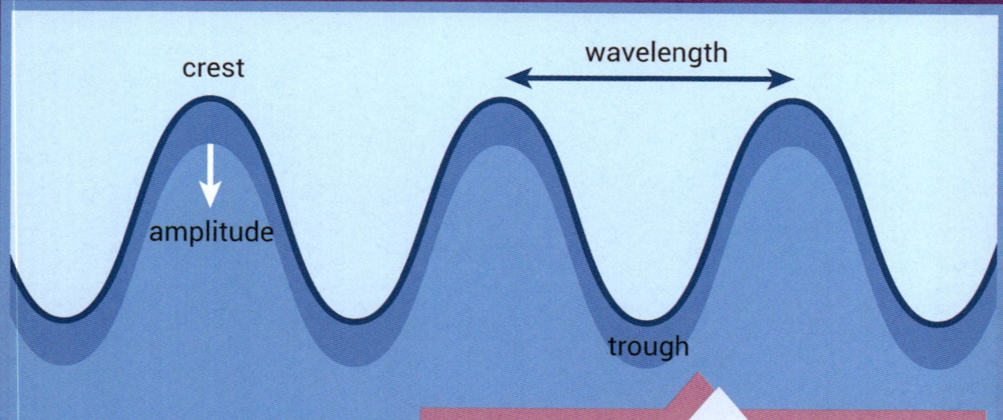

This picture shows the parts of a wave.

FAST FACT

An adult can be knocked off their feet by as little as 6 inches (15 cm) of fast-moving water. Tsunamis can flood an area with as much as 98 feet (30 m) of water.

BEWARE! FAST-MOVING WATER

DEPTH OF MOVING WATER	EFFECTS
6 inches (15.2 cm)	can knock down adults and carry them away
12 inches (30.5 cm)	can carry away small cars
18 to 24 inches (45.7 to 61 cm)	can carry away large vehicles (trucks, vans, SUVs)

WARNING SIGNS

There are a few signs that a tsunami is about to hit. If the trough hits the shore before the crest, the water **recedes** a long way from the shore. This only lasts a few minutes at most before the crest rushes in and sweeps people and things out to sea.

Hearing a loud roar from the ocean is another warning. It may sound like a train or airplane coming closer. Knowing these warning signs could save someone's life.

USE YOUR SENSES

You can use your senses to recognize when a tsunami is about to strike.

- FEEL: Earthquakes make the ground shake.
- SEE: The ocean water drops quickly, exposing the sea floor. This will be followed by a wall of water (the crest of the wave). You may also see people running away from the water.
- HEAR: The wall of water will make a roaring sound similar to a jet plane. You may also hear a tsunami warning siren.
- RUN: Move to higher ground immediately!

Never walk out onto the ocean floor when the water recedes before a tsunami.

ADVANCE WARNING

Sometimes scientists can predict when a tsunami will happen. They can warn people in advance so they can get somewhere safe. Even one minute's warning can make a difference.

Scientists study seismic activity to **predict** tsunamis. They also look at information about the ocean's conditions. If it seems a tsunami is possible, they warn all areas that may be in danger. Some at-risk places notify people through text messages. Tsunami sirens, or alarms, may go off to warn people to get to a safe place.

VERIFIED

The NOAA operates two tsunami warning systems. The Pacific Tsunami Warning Center (PTWC) is located on Ford Island, Hawaii. The National Tsunami Warning Center (NTWC) is located in Palmer, Alaska. To find out more about these warning systems and see warnings about recent seismic activity in the Pacific Ocean visit **www.tsunami.gov**.

This is a **bouy** used by the NOAA to help predict tsunamis.

STAYING SAFE

Learn to recognize the signs that a tsunami is about to hit. If you hear a tsunami siren, get to higher ground right away. Beaches and low-lying areas aren't safe. Since tsunamis can rush miles **inland**, people who can't even see the ocean should still listen to the warning.

FAST FACT

Never stick around to watch a tsunami. If you can see the wave, you're in danger, even on a hill or from the top of a building.

Many places have **evacuation sites** marked so people know they're safe. This tsunami evacuation building is located near Praphat Beach in Thailand.

Find a tall building far from the water and made of sturdy material, such as concrete. Try to find safety by going to the highest point. Most small buildings, such as houses, aren't safe.

If you're near the water when a tsunami comes, never stay to watch it. Run for higher ground as soon as you realize what's happening.

After the tsunami hits, don't return to a coastal area until you've been told it's safe. If you've been given advance warning, make sure there is a radio or TV nearby so you know when you can leave. Don't try to guess! When it's over, stay away from damaged buildings, **debris**, and fallen power lines.

WHAT TO WATCH FOR

There are many dangers to be aware of after a tsunami.

- dangerous debris (nails, glass, bricks, wood, etc.)
- fallen powerlines and utility poles
- fires
- chemical spills
- broken water lines
- broken natural gas lines
- flooding and flash floods
- roaming/lost animals
- roads blocked by fallen trees

VERIFIED

Read more important tips about what to do during and after a tsunami at **www.ready.gov/tsunamis**.

Nails, broken wood, and other sharp objects are a danger after a tsunami.

PLANNING AHEAD

If you live in an area that gets a lot of tsunamis, it's a good idea to have a plan for what to do when one hits. Map out evacuation paths from places where you spend a lot of time, such as home or school. Practice them occasionally.

It's a good idea to put together an **emergency** kit you can take with you. It can include a battery-powered radio, flashlight, food and water, and medicine.

VERIFIED

The U.S. government has a list of things to include in an emergency kit. You can check it out at **www.ready.gov/kit**.

Make sure to include pets in your emergency plan if you have them.

A TSUNAMI HOTSPOT

Some places are more likely to be hit by a tsunami than others. The more tectonic plate movement there is in a certain place, the greater the number of earthquakes that happen there. For example, an area called the Ring of Fire in the Pacific Ocean creates nearly 90 percent of all earthquakes.

This area is home to more than 452 volcanoes that **developed** due to tectonic plate movement. That's 75 percent of all active volcanoes on Earth. That's why it's the place most affected by tsunamis.

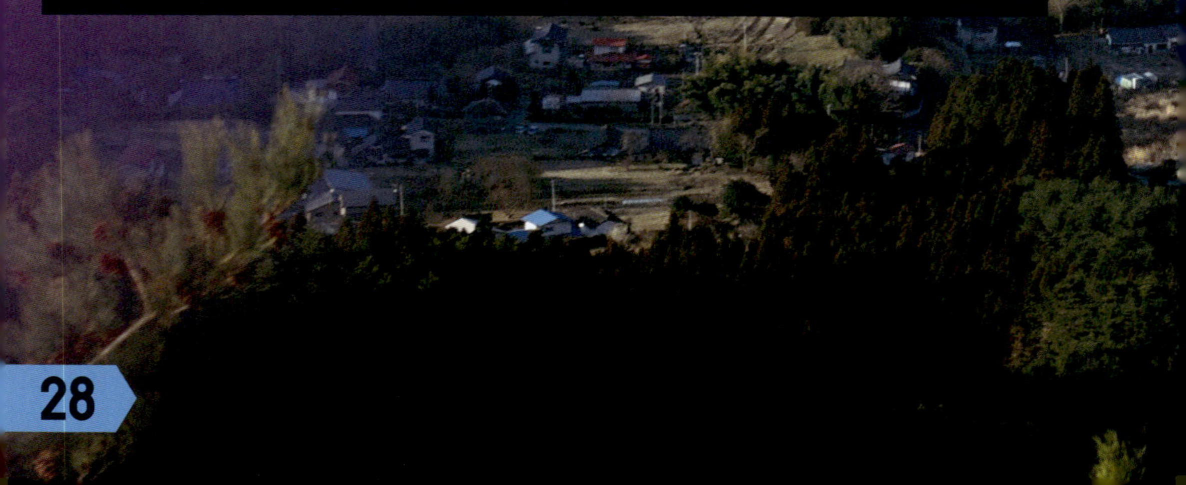

TSUNAMI WARNING STONES

Along the coast of Japan are a series of stones that bear warnings about tsunamis. The oldest of these are about 600 years old. Warnings were carved into the stones for future people. They say things like, "Always be prepared for unexpected tsunamis. Choose life over your possessions and valuables," and "Remember the **calamity** of the great tsunamis. Do not build any homes below this point."

Japan is one of the countries most likely to be hit by a tsunami.

The Ring of Fire is shaped like an upside-down "U." It starts at the southern tip of South America. From there, it travels up the West Coast of North America to the Bering Strait and down past Japan and New Zealand.

People living near the Ring of Fire are always on alert for earthquakes, volcanic eruptions, and tsunamis. Buildings are made in ways that make them less likely to be destroyed by these events. Cities hold earthquake drills so people can practice getting to safety.

Places outside the Ring of Fire rarely or never get tsunamis.

Karymsky volcano, shown here, is one of the most active volcanoes in the world today. It is located on the Ring of Fire on the Kamchatka Peninsula in Russia.

A WALL OF WATER

Tsunamis cause damage in more than one way. When the waves hit the shore, they often push ships miles inland. People and animals on the shore are swept up in the water. If they don't drown, they are often hurt by being pushed along with all the debris in the water, such as cars and trees.

Tsunami waves are very powerful. Each one hits with the force of multiple speeding cars. The waves may continue to slam the shore for hours.

TALLEST TSUNAMI WAVES ON RECORD

LOCATION	DATE	HEIGHT	EVENT THAT CAUSED WAVE
Lituya Bay, Alaska	July 9, 1958	1,720 feet (524 m)	Lituya Bay earthquake
Mount Margaret, Washington	May 18, 1980	820 feet (250 m)	Mt. St. Helens volcano eruption
Piave River valley, Italy	October 9, 1963	771 feet (235 m)	landslide caused by the failed construction of a dam on the Vajont River
Wrangell St.-Elias National Park and Preserve, Alaska	October 17, 2015	633 feet (193 m)	natural landslide in Taan **Fjord**, which is part of Icy Bay, Alaska

Tsunamis are so powerful they can wipe out everything close to shore, including cars, trucks, boats, buildings, and trees.

MAJOR FLOODING

Flooding causes damage to homes and other buildings. This flooding can reach miles away from shore. Telephone lines, power lines, and bridges may break. Power can go out. Flooded streets make it hard for people to get from place to place safely.

Flooded streets make it hard to move around safely.

Floodwater often becomes full of waste, which can spread disease. The floodwater often contaminates, or dirties, drinking water. People can get sick from swallowing it, either on purpose or by accident.

AFTER THE STORM

Tsunamis can keep causing damage even after the waves recede. Pools of standing water attract mosquitos. They can spread diseases such as malaria. People often have trouble finding food or water that isn't contaminated. Some die from not eating or drinking.

Tsunamis are deadly for animals too. Animals may drown, and the places where they live may be ruined. Pollution and waste from the shore may be pulled out into the sea by the receding waves. This harms ocean animals.

FAST FACT

It can take many years for a place to recover after a tsunami. Many people are left homeless. Poor people often don't have the money to fix their home or buy a new one.

Garbage is left on the beach after a tsunami. It is often pulled into the ocean.

REBUILDING TOGETHER

There are a lot of ways people can help after a tsunami. Special teams go to the site of a tsunami as soon as the waves stop. They search through the debris to see if people or animals are trapped and need to be saved.

Doctors help people who've been hurt. People in other countries give money to aid groups to buy fresh food, water, and other items. They hand these out in areas that have been hit by tsunamis.

FAST FACT

It can take years for tsunami damage to be undone. **Volunteers** and government workers spend a long time cleaning and fixing the things the tsunami destroyed.

VERIFIED

Learn how UNICEF helps children after a tsunami at **www.unicefusa.org/mission/emergencies/tsunamis**.

This photo shows volunteers feeding people in Thailand after a tsunami.

HISTORIC TSUNAMIS

Some tsunamis cause more damage than others. The worst tsunami in recorded history happened on December 26, 2004. A powerful earthquake near Sumatra, Indonesia, sent waves in all directions across the Indian Ocean. Many countries were hit. Some of the waves reached 164 feet (50 m).

This tsunami killed about 230,000 people. It reached 3 miles (5 km) inland and caused about $10 billion in damage. Countries created tsunami warning centers to increase notification times.

It took a long time to clean up after the 2004 tsunami.

DEATHS CAUSED BY THE 2004 TSUNAMI

- Indonesia (167,540)
- Sri Lanka (35,322)
- India (16,269)
- Thailand (8,212)
- Somalia (289)
- Maldives (108)
- Malaysia (75)
- Myanmar (61)
- Tanzania (13)
- Bangladesh (2)
- Seychelles (2)
- South Africa (2)
- Yemen (2)
- Kenya (1)

Another destructive tsunami hit Japan on March 11, 2011. It was sparked by one of the strongest earthquakes ever recorded. A 33-foot (10 m) wave slammed into the coastal city of Sendai. One wave rushed about 6 miles (9.7 km) inland.

One of the places hit was Fukushima, the site of a **nuclear** power plant. The tsunami caused explosions at the plant, contaminating the water with nuclear matter. This water leaked into the ocean.

FAST FACT

Nuclear material is deadly to living things. The Fukushima disaster caused many health problems and deaths for Japanese people and wildlife living near the power plant.

Japan suffered damage from both the 2011 tsunami and the earthquake that caused it.

A GROWING DANGER

Tsunamis are natural, but they're also very dangerous. The NOAA reports that tsunamis have killed more than 420,000 people since 1850. Tsunamis also leave many people homeless—sometimes for years. Tsunamis can leave behind disease, **poverty**, and a great sense of loss.

Due to climate change, tsunamis are likely to get worse and more common. Climate change is a change in Earth's weather over a long period of time. Human actions, such as burning **fossil fuels** that pollute the air, cutting down too many trees, and raising more cows and sheep, are making the planet much warmer. This, in turn, is making climate change happen much faster than it normally does.

Cows and sheep release a gas called methane when they burp. This gas traps heat in the air around Earth.

VERIFIED

NASA explains climate change at **climatekids.nasa.gov/climate-change-meaning**.

As the Earth warms up, the ice in the Arctic starts to melt. This adds more water to the oceans, making them rise. A higher water level in the ocean means a tsunami can travel further inland, causing even more damage. Landslides happen more often when frozen soil melts and slides into the ocean. Melting glaciers have caused more earthquakes. People must work together to stop climate change so people all over the world—including those who live in tsunami zones—can stay safe.

GLOSSARY

asteroid: A small, rocky body in space.

basin: In geology, a dip that creates a bowl-like shape in Earth's surface.

bouy: A floating object in a body of water that shows where ships can travel or collects information.

calamity: An event that causes great harm and suffering; a disaster.

damage: Loss or harm caused by injury to a person or piece of property.

debris: Broken pieces of objects.

developed: Created over time.

disturbance: An upset to the natural position or arrangement of something.

emergency: An often-unexpected situation that requires immediate action.

evacuation site: A place where people go for safety during a disaster.

fjord: A narrow inlet of the sea between cliffs or steep slopes.

fossil fuel: A fuel (such as coal, oil, or natural gas) formed in the earth from dead plants or animals.

inland: The part of a country away from the coast.

lithosphere: The outer, solid part of Earth.

nuclear: Having to do with the nucleus of an atom.

poverty: The state of being poor.

predict: To guess what will happen in the future based on facts or knowledge.

pressure: The action of pushing steadily against something.

recede: To move back or away.

rogue: Behaving in an independent, uncontrolled, or dangerous way that is not normal or expected.

seismologist: A person who studies earthquakes.

shallow: Not deep.

volunteer: A person who does something by free choice, usually with no payment expected or given.

INDEX